Remembering
University of Florida Football

Kevin McCarthy

TURNER
PUBLISHING COMPANY

By the 1940s the Gators' football stadium, Florida Field, stood in the midst of athletic facilities that included a baseball field, tennis courts, and a track—all of which allowed students and faculty to spend much of their free time outdoors, exercising and witnessing sporting events in comfort.

Remembering

University of Florida Football

Turner Publishing Company
4507 Charlotte Avenue, Suite 100
Nashville, TN 37209
Phone: (615)255-2665

Remembering University of Florida Football

www.turnerpublishing.com

Library of Congress Control Number: 2011929754

ISBN: 9781596527942

Printed in The United States of America

ISBN: 978-1-68336-899-1 (pbk)

CONTENTS

The first unofficial coach of the football team when the school was in Lake City, Florida, was Professor James Farr (second from left, bottom row, in this 1911 photograph). Farr was also the head of the English Department. The president of the school during the 1901–1902 school term, Dr. T. H. Taliaferro, offered to help Farr in coaching the team if time would allow.

ACKNOWLEDGMENTS

This volume, *Remembering University of Florida Football,* was possible only through the cooperation of University of Florida archivists Carl Van Ness and Joyce Dewsbury. The archives at the Florida Department of State in Tallahassee were also invaluable in the search for old photographs. It is with great thanks and appreciation that we acknowledge the valuable contributions of officials at both institutions for their generous support. The photographs within this volume were chosen from the collections at the University of Florida and at the Florida Department of State and are used by permission.

PREFACE

Football success would have been hard to predict for the University of Florida in its early years, especially after its 1904 team in Lake City was outscored 224–0. Once the school moved to its present location in Gainesville, Florida, it began to do better and then still better, beating a school like Florida Southern 144–0 and holding its own against Southern powerhouses Alabama, Georgia, and Georgia Tech. Like that of many schools, the progress has been slow and often plagued by setbacks, but—with a commitment to excellence in all fields, both academic and athletic—that progress has culminated in a consistently winning program.

The photographs on the following pages trace the history of football to what is today one of the true bastions of gridiron superiority. They point out how UF has won three national championships in the last three decades, has produced three Heisman Trophy winners, and has sent forth hundreds of ballplayers to excel in the National Football League and, even more important, in the fields of business, education, law, medicine, religion, and service.

These images have been selected from archives in Gainesville and Tallahassee and have been captioned with short explanations describing the scenes depicted. With the exception of touching up imperfections that have accrued with the passage of time and cropping where necessary, no changes have been made. The focus and clarity of many images are limited to the technology and the ability of the photographer at the time they were recorded. In many cases, the photos have not been seen by the public for decades, if ever. Now with the Gator Nation exceeding 250,000 living alumni and with the student body more than 50,000, interest in all things associated with the University of Florida is high.

While many people around the nation and world associate the University of Florida with the Fightin' Gators, it is my fondest hope that interest in the football program will extend to interest in the school's many academic accomplishments, and that pride in being associated with the school will lead to even more highly qualified students studying there, adding to the number of alumni and friends supporting the institution's many efforts to make this world a better place to live.

As the state's oldest, largest, and most comprehensive university, the University of Florida is also the nation's fourth-largest. Its more than 50,000 students study in ideal surroundings of more than 2,000 acres in a city that prides itself on beauty and culture. The athletic teams in general, and the football program in particular, have done much to put UF on the sports map. In fact, only UF and UCLA appear in the top ten in each of the last 25 national all-sports rankings. More important, UF's 89 percent graduation rate among athletes in recent years has made clear to students and alumni alike how important the college diploma is. The high demands that the more than 4,000 faculty place on the students, including the athletes, ensure that a UF degree is a valuable commodity in preparing them for the post-school world.

Here then is the story of the many successes and some failures of the storied UF football program, how the tears of desperation in the early years have consistently given way to the euphoria associated with high rankings and victories.

—Kevin McCarthy

The town of Gainesville, which had been established in 1854, was incorporated in 1869, four years after the Civil War ended. By 1884, when this sketch was made, the town had about 2,000 residents, along with fourteen cotton gins, three railroads, and many citrus and vegetable farms. What it did not have was a college or university. Those interested in a higher education looked to Lake City to the north, which did have a university.

Early Roads to Gridiron Greatness

(1853–1929)

Another predecessor of UF and of the Gator football team was the team fielded by East Florida Seminary (EFS) in Gainesville, shown here in 1902. The school opened in 1854 in Ocala, but moved north to Gainesville in 1866, after the Civil War. It had 71 students in 1866 and 225 in 1904. The football team played other Florida schools.

Roy Corbett, captain of the 1907 Gator team. He claimed that he was the first student to register at the new University of Florida when it opened for classes in Gainesville in 1906. Players on those early teams were given a jersey and pants, but had to provide their own shoes, headgear (if they chose to wear it), and all protective clothing.

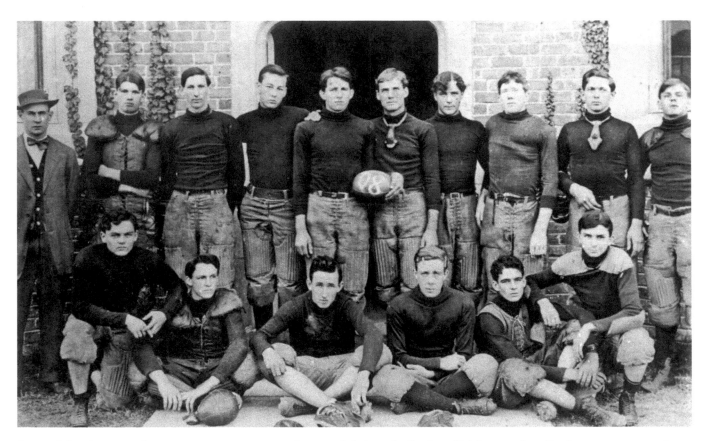

Some of the players on the 1908 team wear nose guards around their necks for the official group shot. Equipment was sparse in those days, and some players refused to wear the helmets, which—though made only of leather—added some protection for their heads. The coach in those early games was James "Pee Wee" Forsythe, who coached for three seasons (1906–1908), enjoying a 14-6-2 record.

In a 1908 game against Jacksonville's Riverside Athletic Club in South Jacksonville, the Gators won 4–0 at a time when both touchdowns and field goals counted for 4 points. Spectators in their finest outfits stand along the sidelines, long before stadium seating with skyboxes and replay screens. The Gators beat the Athletic Club in each of the six matches they played against each other.

The 1912 team also posed with President Murphree. As president from 1909 to 1927, a crucial time in the history of the young school, Murphree did much to put UF on the road to excellence in many fields. Of American football, he noted that the sport "develops intuition, cultivates mental alertness, self-control, and physical manhood."

In 1912, education officials awarded the university with a contract for the construction of Floyd Hall, a three-story building that would house the College of Agriculture, in which the building's namesake, Major Wilbur Floyd, was assistant dean (1915–1938). During the 1918 Spanish influenza epidemic that swept the country and the UF campus, Floyd Hall was converted into a temporary hospital. The building was restored in 1992 and renamed Griffin-Floyd Hall, also for alumnus Ben Hill Griffin, Jr.

The freshmen football players at UF, who were not allowed to compete against the varsity, played their own schedule against out-of-town opponents. In the 1920s, they did so well one season, going undefeated, that the UF yearbook labeled them "Champions of the South."

En route to playing and losing to Harvard, 24–0, in Massachusetts, the 1922 Gator team stopped off in Washington, D.C., where they toured the city and Capitol and then visited the White House. Shown here at the White House, the players and coaches shook hands with President Warren Harding, whom they cheered loudly, since it was his birthday.

Early Gator home games, like this one between the Gators and Mercer College, were played on Fleming Field, which today can be found between West University Avenue and the stadium. The university baseball team also used Fleming Field, as did professional baseball teams like the Boston Red Sox and New York Giants. The Gators played Mercer 17 times between 1906 and 1928 and racked up a 10-6-1 record against them.

Robert "Ark" Newton, pictured here running off-tackle, arrived at UF in 1921 from his native Arkansas (hence his nickname) and became a member of the football team, after Coach Van Fleet saw him kick a 60-yard punt. In one game, he kicked a 92-yard punt. Newton was also a strong runner and receiver.

Because freshmen were not allowed to compete against varsity teams in the Southern Conference, they had their own intercollegiate schedule. The "Baby Gators" went undefeated in 1926 and were called "Champions of the South" at a time when the Gator varsity had a poor 2-6-2 record, the only time that decade that they did poorly.

The Great Depression had many effects on UF, including scaling back the grandiose plans involving University Auditorium, built in 1927. Even at that, the auditorium became the center of campus, especially after the 1953 construction of the nearby Century Tower, with its magnificent carillon at the top. For many years, at the base of the tower was a pen that enclosed a live alligator.

The 1928 Gators led the nation in scoring, totaling 336 points to their opponents' 44 and beating Georgia for the first time. UF's only loss that 8-1 season was to Tennessee on a soggy field in Nashville, a game in which some Gator fans thought the groundskeeper had soaked the gridiron to slow down the high-scoring Florida team.

One of the most lopsided victories of the 1928 season, or any season, was the 71–6 victory over Sewanee in Jacksonville in November. This photo shows Gator runner Goodbread on a 24-yard touchdown run. After the first three games, all the rest were away, including Jacksonville, Savannah, and Knoxville. Florida won seven of the nine games played against Sewanee, a rivalry reaching back to 1914.

These women at a Florida homecoming game in the late 1920s were part of a long-continuing tradition, begun in 1924, of having graduates return to campus, renew acquaintances, attend a football game, and brag of their success. They would be introduced during halftime in pageantry that became more and more elaborate each year.

Coach Charles Bachman (at far left) was the eighth head coach of the Gators. Over his five seasons (1928–1932), he built a 27-18-3 record and was the first Gator coach to be inducted into the National Football Foundation and the College Hall of Fame. He later became the football coach at Michigan State University for 14 years.

Early broadcasters of Gator games sat between the fans and the gridiron. Seen behind these four announcers at a 1928 game are (left to right, beginning with the third person in from the left) Governor Doyle Carlton, Mrs. John Tigert, Senator Duncan Fletcher, Mrs. Doyle Carlton, and UF president John Tigert.

The year 1929 was hard in Florida, with the stock market crash and diseases that wiped out the orange crop, but at least exciting football games took the minds of many off the serious problems facing the country. UF's 1929 team triumphed with an 8-2 record, including a victory over Oregon in Miami, the first time the Gators had played a West Coast team.

Florida Field was dedicated on November 30, 1930. Nearly 22,000 fans attended the first home game, a loss to Alabama 20–0, in a facility that would be expanded as the team improved. The announcer for the game was a UF student, the famous Red Barber, who would become a baseball announcer for the Reds, Dodgers, and Yankees.

A New Stadium and Hard Times

(1930–1945)

The 1930 homecoming game against Alabama ended up a Florida loss, but at least the women in the Homecoming Court and their ROTC escorts had good seats near the field. That loss was only one of three for the Gators that season. They finished with a 6-3-1 record, outscoring their opponents 198–61. The one tie was a 0–0 defensive match against the hated Bulldogs of Georgia.

End Ed Parnell of Stuart (no. 85 in the first row), who captained the 1931 football team, received honorable mention on the All-Southern Conference team in a year when the Gators had a disappointing 2-6-2 record. The decade would not be good for Florida football, which finished the ten years with a poor 42-52-6 record.

The Gators kept the game ball showing their victory against North Carolina State, 34–0, in 1931. The Gators traveled a lot that season, going to North Carolina, New York, Alabama, and California to play their games. Such travel to out-of-state, hostile stadia gave them good experience and also allowed local high school players to see the kind of football played by the Gators.

On October 31, 1931, the Georgia Bulldogs played the Gators at Florida Field for the first time, defeating them 33–6. The Bulldogs would not return to Gainesville until 1994, when the stadium in Jacksonville, where the two teams usually played each other, was being renovated for the NFL's Jacksonville Jaguars.

Cheerleaders in the 1930s were all white males at a time when the university did not have any African-American or female students. The six students pictured here also served as the executive committee for the Gator Pep Club. The cheerleaders were usually skilled gymnasts who could leap and do breathtaking cartwheels.

Many students, including athletes, went to the campus infirmary for minor aches and bruises, colds, and shots. The building, officially known as the Students Health Center, opened in 1931. In later years Shands Hospital, down the hill from the campus, would treat the more serious illnesses among students.

In October 1934, two American Legion officers joined Governor David Sholtz (second from left) and UF president John Tigert (third from left) to dedicate a plaque on the north wall of Florida Field during the Tulane game. A scroll behind the plaque listed those Floridians killed during World War I.

Despite a well-maintained playing field and enthusiastic crowds on game days, the Gators did so poorly in the last half of the thirties that Coach Josh Cody, the school's tenth head coach, could manage only a 17-24-2 record over four seasons (1936–1939). Cody would become one of six coaches hired to lead the Gators in the 1930s and '40s.

The so-called Freshman Pep Squad sat together at football games in the 1930s. Over the years various customs involved all the freshmen—for example, saying "hello" to everyone they met on campus, memorizing the names of university and student government officials, and not taking shortcuts across the Plaza but using only the sidewalks and roads. The cheerleaders would sometimes call all the freshmen out to join in impromptu pep rallies and pajama parades.

Workers installed lights in the football stadium in the late 1930s, thanks to a generous donation from Georgia Seagle, a strong supporter of the university. The lights enabled homecoming events (as pictured here) and, later, football games to take place in the cool of the evening, thus avoiding daytime heat and humidity, although Gator teams were hardened to such conditions.

The annual game against the Georgia Bulldogs, usually played in neutral Jacksonville, is one of the fiercest rivalries in the Southeast, especially because both teams are in the same division of the Southeastern Conference and their game is usually held late in the season, when the division championship is on the line.

Photos of cheerleaders appeared in the school's annual yearbook, *Seminole,* which students produced from 1910 until 1973 and then again beginning in 1983 with a new name, *The Tower,* to prevent confusion with Florida State University in Tallahassee, which had a Seminole Indian as its mascot.

In 1943, UF president John Tigert (at left) and Dean Harold Hume of the College of Agriculture rode onto Florida Field in style. That year the Gators, like many college teams in America, did not field a football team, because World War II was in progress. Many male students were drafted during the war, and seven UF football players were killed in action.

Postwar Success

(1946–1969)

In 1946, after World War II and before large numbers of veterans arrived to help, UF suffered its worst season ever, going 0-9-0. In this game against Villanova, the Gators lost 27–20 at home. Not until Charley Pell's first year as head coach (1979), when the Gators lost all ten games (though tying one) would the year again be as bad.

In 1947, two years after World War II ended and after thousands of soldiers returned home, many armed services personnel, both men and women, wanted to take advantage of the G. I. Bill, which enabled them to attend college. UF became coeducational, and the athletic teams recruited men and women to lead the cheers.

The Fighting Gator Band became a regular fixture at football games in the late 1940s and led the fans in rousing fight songs. UF's band had a proud tradition of service, dating back to 1917, when the U.S. entered World War I against Germany. When the worldwide conflict erupted, the university band joined the war effort as a unit, becoming the 124th Infantry Band.

Coach Raymond "Bear" Wolf, head football coach for four seasons (1946–1949), welcomed many older players as returning veterans joined the team. The Florida legislature helped fund athletic scholarships to UF through tax revenues generated from pari-mutuel betting at racetracks and jai-alai frontons in the state.

The small scoreboard in the south end zone lasted from the 1930s to the 1960s, but would later be replaced with a huge sign that gave much information about downs, yards to first down, time-outs, and total statistics. Workers would later add temporary bleachers to the south end zone to increase its capacity to more than 62,000.

One of Coach Wolf's best players was Chuck Hunsinger (no. 46), who started for the Gators for four years (1946–1949) and had some great moments, among them winning SEC Back of the Week for the 1949 Gator victory over Georgia. He was part of a surprisingly intact squad that stayed together for three years (1946–1948) and had a role in a great upset: a 7–6 win over North Carolina State in 1947.

Chuck Hunsinger (no. 46) was very popular with the fans and was willing to sign autographs after a game.

Beginning in 1949, George Edmondson, Jr., of Tampa, Florida, better known as Mr. Two Bits, would go to the center of Florida Field dressed in his yellow shirt with orange-and-blue tie and lead the crowd in a "two bits" cheer.

Coach Wolf is shown here with Fred Montsdeoca on the left and Jimmy Kynes on the right in 1949. Kynes, UF's first All-SEC lineman, was the last Gator player to play 60 minutes in a football game and, in fact, averaged 55 minutes a game that season. Measuring a big 6 feet 3 inches, 204 pounds, Kynes, who lettered for four years (1946–1949), became a lawyer and in 1964 the youngest Attorney General of Florida.

In a game against Auburn that ended in a tie in Mobile, Alabama, in Coach Wolf's last season as head coach (1949), he is seen speaking with 21-year-old end Fal Johnson of Gainesville. Many of the players were in their mid-20s, having served as soldiers in World War II. Alumni pressure at the end of the 1949 season led to Wolf's resignation, to be replaced in 1950 by Bob Woodruff.

Choosing an alligator for mascot, shown here in an early form, turned out to be a pretty good idea. It would give rise to things like a nickname for Florida Field. In the 1990s, the stadium was dubbed "the Swamp," the place where gators live and eat animals like bulldogs and wildcats.

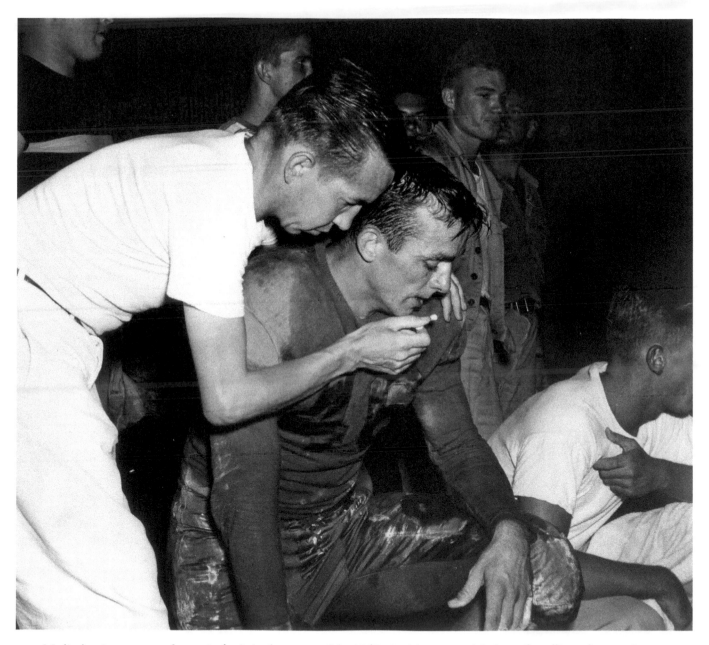

Medical assistance was often quite basic in the games of the 1940s, in this case a quick dose of smelling salts to revive a woozy Gator. The lack of strong, protective gear led to more injuries than in games today, and some players, like Jimmy Kynes, played all 60 minutes of a game, a tactic that could exhaust the less physically fit.

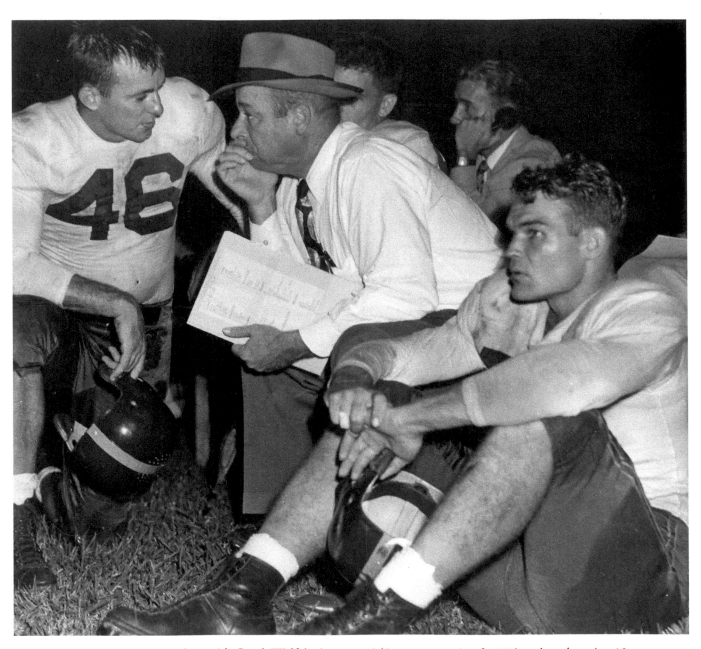

Chuck Hunsinger (no. 46), seen here with Coach Wolf, had a great 1949 season, running for 774 yards and scoring 12 touchdowns. He was so good that an Alabama reporter composed "The Hunsinger Song" about him with these words: "Hunsinger the Humdinger you ought to see him go!" After college, the Chicago Bears drafted him in the first round for the NFL.

The 1949 win against Georgia, 28–7, ended a seven-game losing streak against what has consistently been one of the fiercest rivals of the Gators. Coach Wolf's players carried their beleaguered coach off the field on their shoulders before 27,000 fans in Jacksonville. It would be Wolf's last victory in his last season, which ended at 4-5-1. His four-season record was a disappointing 13-24-2.

The Fightin' Gator Band, which attended all home games and many away games, would grow from several dozen to more than one hundred musicians.

An aerial view of the UF campus in the late 1940s shows the football field in the middle of a track field, baseball diamond, tennis courts, gymnasium, and a newly begun Florida Gym, where the basketball team would play for 31 seasons (1949–1980). Generous benefactors donated money for the installation of lights around the football field and for the construction of off-campus housing for the athletes.

The main library, pictured here in 1949, remained one of the centerpieces of a beautiful campus. The success of the football team helped the library in later, leaner years when the Athletic Association donated to the library some of the money earned in bowl games, thus allowing all the students to benefit from the success of the team on the field.

Adding upper levels to the stadium in 1950 ushered in the Bob Woodruff decade as the school's 13th head coach. He built a record of 53-2-6 in ten seasons, led UF to its first-ever bowl game (a victory over Tulsa in the 1952 Gator Bowl), beat the Georgia Bulldogs six of ten games, and started the UF-FSU rivalry.

Students in the stands have always enjoyed participation, such as performing card pictures at the command of an announcer. These pictures faced the alumni, who sat in the shaded section of the stadium, with a view of the pictures like that of the photographer.

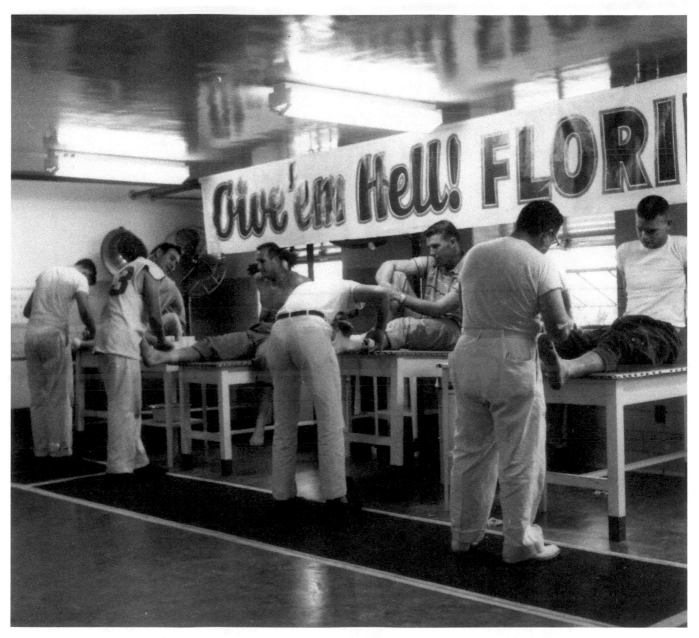

The '50s saw a growing awareness of good training, eating, and exercise. Head trainer Sam Lankford (at far right) and his staff are shown here taping the ankles of players for an early morning practice before the student-athletes head to class. The training room in the Florida Gym would eventually become state-of-the-art.

One of the new traditions in the Coach Woodruff era was the ringing of the so-called Victory Bell after an important win, for example the 1950 win over Vanderbilt. The bell was salvaged from the USS *Florida,* a battleship commissioned in 1911 and scrapped in 1932. Officials placed the bell in the Hub, the bookstore which was in the center of campus.

The sidelines of football fields during the 1940s and '50s slowly became better equipped to handle the physical bruises and injuries suffered by the players. Equipment included oxygen masks and liniments, to help prevent serious injuries.

The 1950 team had three quarterbacks: (from left to right) Haywood Sullivan, Angus Williams, and Kent Stevens. The 6-foot-4-inch Sullivan became the first sophomore in the SEC to pass for more than 1,000 yards. The Boston Red Sox baseball team signed him after his sophomore season with a $75,000 bonus, and he left for the pros.

Jacksonville's Gator Bowl has been a favorite out-of-town place for the Gators to play. The Gators played eight bowl games there between 1953 and 1999, winning six times, including the school's first bowl ever, the 1953 win over Tulsa.

The homecoming parade, held the day before the big football game, proceeded east on University Avenue from the stadium to the center of town. Thousands of spectators lined both sides of the street to see the bands, floats, and personages, such as Miss Florida for 1954, who waves to the crowd from a convertible.

The 1956 Gators, pictured here in their coats and ties, held a very good 6-3-1 record, a 28–0 thrashing of Georgia, a five-game winning streak, and a national ranking of number 12. The five-game winning streak was the longest up to that time following the eight straight wins of the 1928 team, the one that led the nation in scoring.

Defensive guard John Barrow, a first-team All American, was also the SEC Lineman of the Year in 1956. After UF, he played football for 15 seasons in the Canadian Football League and then became general manager at Toronto. As would frequently happen at UF, his son, Greg, joined the team and lettered as a tackle in 1980.

A live alligator has occasionally come out of the waters on campus and wandered around, much to the delight of students and broadcasters in town, in this instance for an episode of the *Hootenanny* TV show. Lake Alice, just south of the football stadium, is still a favorite swimming hole for the animals.

An aerial view of the UF campus from the late 1950s reveals its great size, with the athletic fields concentrated on the western edges and the health center to the south.

After much reluctance on the part of UF officials, and at the urging of both state legislators and Governor Leroy Collins, UF agreed to play the new Seminoles team of Florida State University in 1958 in Gainesville. The program cover for the first game implied a friendliness that was not present on the field.

The 1960s at UF saw the hiring of a new head coach, the beloved Ray Graves, who instituted a powerful offense, recruited the school's first Heisman Trophy winner (Steve Spurrier), and established a winning tradition at the school with a record of 70-31-4 that decade. He took the Gators to five bowl games, winning four of them.

Cheerleaders in a 1960 home game at Florida Field found a new use for their megaphones. In later years, fans in the stands would not be allowed to use umbrellas, which could drip water on nearby spectators and could be used to smuggle in liquor.

The equipment in the press box in the early 1960s was basic: a microphone, telephone, binoculars, stat sheet, and food. In later years, the press box would be enclosed and have state-of-the-art facilities.

UF quarterback Larry Libertore, who weighed just 135 pounds, passes over an FSU defender blocked by fullback Don Goodman (no. 45). "Little Larry" Libertore, a cagey option runner-passer, led the Gators to a record nine wins in 1960. When Tommy Shannon replaced Larry as signal caller, Larry became a defensive back.

In his first season as head coach, Ray Graves took his team to play Baylor in the 1960 Gator Bowl in Jacksonville. Their victory was the first of four bowl games his team won that decade. The pageantry of the bowl games as pictured here played well on television and for the fans there in person.

Three lovely coeds pretend to corral a gator on campus. Among the very few other schools that used an alligator for a mascot were Allegheny College in Pennsylvania, San Jacinto College in Texas, San Francisco State University in California, and Green River Community College in Washington. The original mascot of San Francisco State University was the Golden Gate Bridge, and the teams were nicknamed the "Gaters," which eventually became the "Gators."

Ray Graves posed with his coaches and team during the 1962 season, one that ended with a 7-4 record, including a 17–7 win over Lambert Trophy winner and eastern football power Penn State in the Gator Bowl. During that season Coach Graves heard from his brother in Knoxville, Tennessee, about a local young man up there who would put Gator football on the map to stay: Steve Spurrier.

Coach Graves, seen here talking with quarterback Mike McVay (no. 16) and halfback Don Deal (no. 21) during a game in the early 1960s, had much experience in football, having played at Tennessee in college and then with the Philadelphia Eagles in the NFL and having coached at Tennessee and Georgia Tech.

What had to be one of the least fearsome of gator outfits was used in the early 1960s by the UF cheerleaders. How UF became the Gators dates back to 1908, when a local Gainesville merchant was visiting his son in Virginia, wanted to have pennants made for UF's team, decided on an alligator because of its association with Florida, and the rest is history.

In 1964, Larry Dupree became the first Gator running back to earn first-team All-American honors. His 1,725 rushing yards in three years is one of the highest totals ever for a Gator. He was the captain of the 1964 team, which posted a 7-4 record, scored 181 points, and held their opponents to only 98.

In a 1964 game, quarterback Steve Spurrier (no. 11) ran behind Larry Beckman (no. 66), Marquis Baeszler (no. 34), Randy Jackson (no. 88), Bill Carr (no. 51), and Jim Benson (no. 60). Beckman, Benson, Carr, and Spurrier each made the All-SEC team at least once in their careers at Florida. Spurrier won the 1966 Heisman Trophy—the first Gator to do so.

After Franklin "Pepper" Rodgers (to the left of Coach Ray Graves in this photo) served as an assistant coach at UF, he went on to become the head coach at the University of Kansas, UCLA, and Georgia Tech. At Kansas he led the team to the 1968 Big 8 championship. He also coached the Memphis Showboats of the United States Football League.

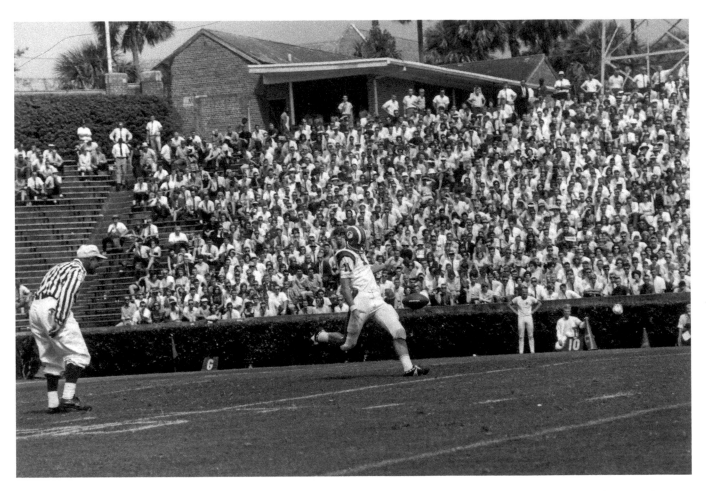

Steve Spurrier was not only a great quarterback, but also an effective kicker. Seen here kicking a punt against Southern Methodist University in the first game of the 1964 season, he is well known for the winning, 40-yard field goal against Auburn in 1966, effectively clinching the Heisman Trophy as a senior.

Steve Spurrier finished the 1965 season by being named the most outstanding player in the Sugar Bowl, the first time a player from the losing team had won that honor. He broke six bowl records in that game, a 20–18 loss to Missouri. The following season he helped the Gators beat Auburn by kicking a field goal near the end of the game.

In a clever publicity shot, the photographer put Spurrier the player on the shoulders of two of his coaches, whereas normally the players carried their successful coach off the field after a great victory.

Bill Carr lettered at UF for three years (1964–1966), started at center in 32 consecutive games, and earned All-American honors in his senior season. The New Orleans Saints in the NFL later drafted him, but an ROTC commitment prevailed and he served in the U.S. Army in Korea. Carr became UF's athletic director from 1980 to 1986.

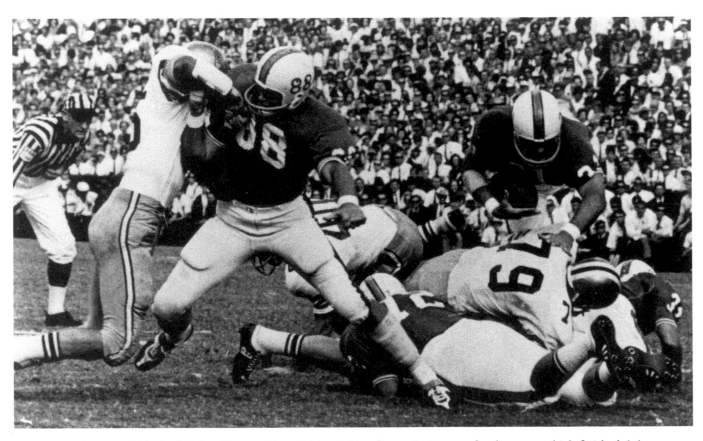

Jim Yarbrough (no. 88) blocks for Tom Christian (no. 31) in 1967, a disappointing year for the team, which finished 6-4. Yarbrough lettered for three years (1966–1968), was named to UF's Team of the Century as a tight end, and later played in the NFL (1969–1977) as an offensive tackle for the Detroit Lions and Houston Oilers.

In the 1967 Orange Bowl in Miami, the Gators beat Georgia Tech 27–12 in the final game against the Yellow Jackets coached by Bobby Dodd (the former coach of Ray Graves). Gator tailback Larry Smith rushed for a 94-yard touchdown, still a record for the Orange Bowl. Smith rushed for 187 yards that day and was named the MVP of the game.

On the third offensive play of the 1969 season, UF quarterback John Reaves threw a touchdown pass to fellow sophomore Carlos Alvarez, starting a 9-1-1 season in which the Gators scored 329 points, the second-highest record in UF history to that time, while holding opponents to just 187. It would be the end of a great decade of Florida football.

Carlos Alvarez, nicknamed the "Cuban Comet," set Gator football records that stood for decades. His first Gator reception from John Reaves on the third play of the opening game against Houston, which had been ranked number one in the pre-season, was for a touchdown in a lopsided UF victory, 59–34.

By the 1960s, the equipment on the sidelines had become better organized and complete as the teams grew in size and as medical doctors stood by in case of an emergency.

PADS
Thigh Caps
Humerus Pads
KNEE BRACE
Thigh CAPS
NECK ROLL

PADS -
Hit-Away
Rib
Cosby Bruise

TAPE
ELASTIC WRAPS
FELT-FOAM
BACK PLASTERS
SLINGS

DISAPPOINTMENTS AND TRIUMPHS

(1970–1996)

Florida Field, which was becoming one of the finest facilities for football games in the Southeast, saw a different style of play in the 1970s. The wide-open, passing offense of Ray Graves in the 1960s became more of a running game as new coach Doug Dickey introduced the wishbone offense. The 1960s would be missed by Florida fans.

Guard Burton Lawless lettered at UF for three years (1972–1974), became a first-team All American (1974), and was named to UF's Team of the Century. After UF, he played for the Cowboys (1975–1979), the Lions (1980), and the Dolphins (1981) in the NFL.

The school's band grew larger and larger over the years until it included more than a hundred performers, baton girls, and flag wavers. By the 1970s, members spent much time practicing and could often be heard for a mile or so around the stadium early on home-game days.

Coach Dickey's first win as the head coach was against Duke in Jacksonville, 21–19. The closeness of the contest caused much consternation on the sidelines as is clear from the looks on the faces of these coeds.

Jack Youngblood (no. 74), considered by many to be UF's best defensive end, was a first-team All-American player in 1970. After his Gator career, he was drafted by the NFL's Los Angeles Rams in the first round and played his entire career with that team (1971–1984). He was an All-Pro seven times and is best known for playing in Super Bowl XIV with a broken leg.

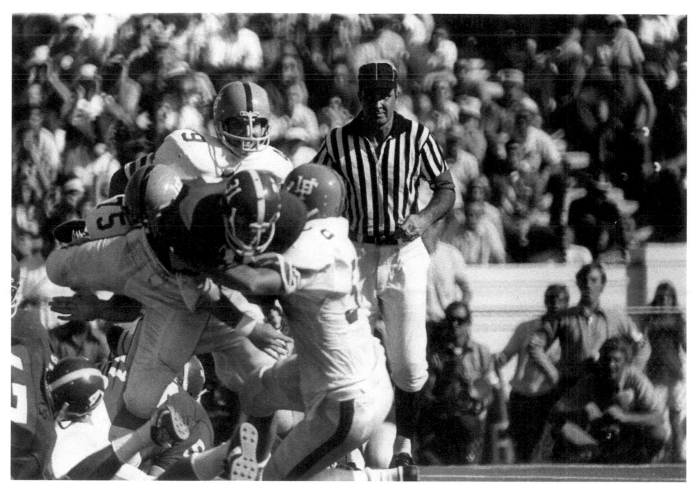

Coach Dickey's first loss as the head coach was in Tuscaloosa against the Crimson Tide of Alabama, 46–15. He would go on to a 7-4 record that season, but the losses were against SEC rivals Alabama, Tennessee, and Auburn, as well as the independent Miami.

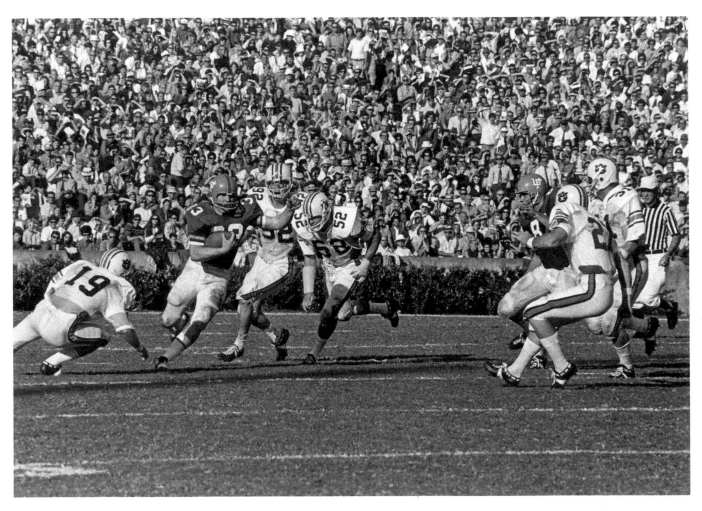

Tommy Durrance (no. 33) was a three-year starter at halfback for the Gators (1969–1971) and a good transition from the Graves era to the Dickey era. He led the team in rushing for two seasons, scored a record 30 touchdowns in his career (thus his nickname "Touchdown Tommy"), and was the unanimous choice to be captain of the 1971 team.

A transfer from Miami-Dade Junior College, Nat Moore set the UF rushing record in 1972 with 145 carries for 845 yards and 9 touchdowns. As a senior he broke his knee early in the next season, but returned to his great form when he carried the ball against FSU 15 times for 109 yards in a 49–0 rout of the Seminoles, the worst defeat that team had ever suffered.

Gator senior and team captain Fred Abbott (no. 68) joined Ricky Browne (no. 50), Clint Griffin (no. 78), and Mike Moore (no. 85) in harassing opposing quarterbacks during the 1972 season, in this case FSU quarterback Gary Huff (no. 19). The thrashing they gave to FSU that year, 42–13, was one of the largest margins of victory in the UF-FSU series. In fact, Florida's first 35 points were the result of FSU fumbles and miscues.

Coach Ray Graves, who stepped down as head coach of the Gators in 1970 to become UF's athletic director, brought a care and benevolence to his players that they responded to with reciprocity. His players from the foregoing decade bonded so closely that they have continued to meet annually for a "Silver Sixties" reunion.

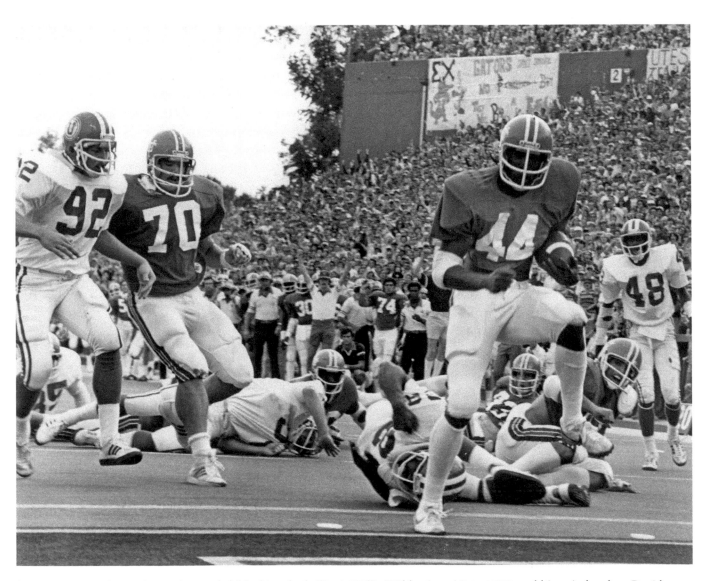

Dennis Forrester (no. 70), seen here at left blocking for halfback Willie Wilder (no. 44) in 1978, and his twin brother, David Forrester, both of whom lettered for three years (1975–1977), anchored a strong offensive line. There would be other twin brothers who played for the Gators over the years.

Coach Ray Graves (at left) escorted New York Yankees' owner George Steinbrenner onto Florida Field in 1978. Steinbrenner was a strong supporter of Gator athletics, including football and baseball, and helped fund improvements to the athletic facilities.

Yancey Sutton lettered for the Gators in football (1978–1980) while playing for two UF coaches: Doug Dickey and Charley Pell. He refused to let his deafness hold him back and went on to become a professional golfer after college.

Dwayne Dixon (no. 83) lettered at UF (1980–1983) before going on to play in the NFL (1984–1985, 1987) and the Arena Football League (1987–1991), where he had the unusual distinction of twice winning the prestigious "Iron Man" award for his skills. He also coached UF's wide receivers in the 1990s.

Doug Dickey, who had grown up in Gainesville and played quarterback for the Gators (1952–1953), became the team's 15th head coach in 1970. He held the post for nine years (1970–1978), compiling a 58-43-2 record before becoming the athletic director at the University of Tennessee. He was inducted into the National Football Foundation Hall of Fame in 2004.

In an ongoing evolution of the gator mascot, this particular one featured a rather mild reptile costume. The problem was that temperatures inside the outfit could surpass one hundred degrees. The mascot, which does not talk and therefore has to mime a lot, would later become Albert the Alligator and be joined by Alberta.

The large scoreboard at the north end zone was a far cry from the puny one at the south end zone, which stood from the 1930s to the 1960s. Florida Field's capacity had been increased to 62,800 in 1966 and would become even larger as the teams continued to excel. It would also be known as one of the noisiest stadia in the country.

In 1979, school officials had the Stephen C. O'Connell Center for basketball, nicknamed the O'Dome, built near the football stadium. Both would see their teams win national championships in the decade of the 1990s and would be the scene of graduations, concerts, political rallies, and Gator Growl, the student-run extravaganza held the night before the homecoming game. The first-rate facilities for football and basketball helped recruit star athletes to the university.

"Passing up" a fan in the stands became a favorite activity on the student side of the stadium in the 1970s. The students sat on the north side, facing the sun, so they usually wore comfortable, even skimpy clothes, unlike fans in the past, when alumni and students alike dressed up for the weekly games.

Coaches like Charley Pell stressed conditioning of the players, hired strength coaches, and conditioned the team for the difficulty of playing in the heat and humidity of Florida Field. When the Gators lost to bigger teams like Nebraska, the coaches recruited larger players who could hold their own on the line. Coaches Spurrier and Meyer also stressed speed among the receivers.

The 1980 Gator win over Maryland in the Tangerine Bowl, 35–20, ended a remarkable 8-4 season after the disastrous 0-10-1 1979 season.

One of the most effective Gator quarterbacks of the 1980s was Wayne Peace (no. 15), whose 1982 70.3 percent completion rate broke the NCAA single-season record. He and the other UF quarterback, Bob Hewko, led the team to an 8-4 record that year, achieved with strong runners like Neal Anderson, James Jones, and John L. Williams, as well as a strong defense with stars like Wilber Marshall.

In their quest to build up the strength and stamina of the players, the football coaches had a new weight room built.

Among the Gator players chosen to the 24-member SEC All-Academic team in the early 1980s for their scholastic success were (clockwise) kicker Brian Clark (no. 3), nose guard Robin Fisher (no. 66), wide receiver Spencer Jackson III (no. 89), wide receiver Broughton Lang (no. 2), quarterback Wayne Peace (no. 15), guard Dan Plonk (no. 65), and defensive back Vito McKeever (no. 36).

UF fans tore down the goalpost at Florida Field after the Gators defeated the Seminoles 35–3 behind the pinpoint passing of Wayne Peace, who completed 20 of 33 passes with four touchdowns. It was UF Coach Charley Pell's first victory in the UF-FSU series, and one that he himself called his "greatest win."

Wilber Marshall (no. 88), seen here returning an interception, was named to the first-team All-SEC three consecutive years (1981–1983), All American (1982 and 1983), and nation's "Defensive Player of the Year" by ABC-TV (1983). The Chicago Bears picked him in the first round, and he played 12 seasons in the NFL for five different teams, becoming All-Pro three times (1986, 1987, 1992).

Albert (at left) and Alberta were photographed in 1983 standing in front of an alligator prop used in a movie. Other schools have used the alligator as a mascot, among them Allegheny College, Green River Community College, San Francisco State University, and San Jacinto College, but UF has become the school most closely associated with the reptile. Thousands of fans have done the Gator Chomp at Florida Field to intimidate foes.

Fullback John L. Williams (no. 22) threw a block for quarterback Wayne Peace (no. 15) in a 1983 game against the Seminoles. Williams was the first Gator player to rush for more than 2,000 yards and catch passes for more than 700 yards (1982–1985). The NFL Seattle Seahawks drafted him in the first round (1986). Williams played for them (1986–1993) and for the Pittsburgh Steelers (1994–1995).

Head Coach Charley Pell races out onto Florida Field between offensive star Lorenzo Hampton (no. 7) and defensive star Wilber Marshall (no. 88) in 1983. The next year, tailback Hampton caught a 54-yard touchdown pass from Kerwin Bell against Tulane, beginning a string of eight consecutive wins that year.

One assistant coach at Florida in the 1980s who went on to the NFL was Mike Shanahan, offensive coordinator for four years (1980–1983). During that stretch, the Gators went to four bowl games, two of which they won. He became the head coach of the Los Angeles Raiders (1988–1989) and later the Denver Broncos (1995–2008), where he won back-to-back Super Bowls (1998, 1999).

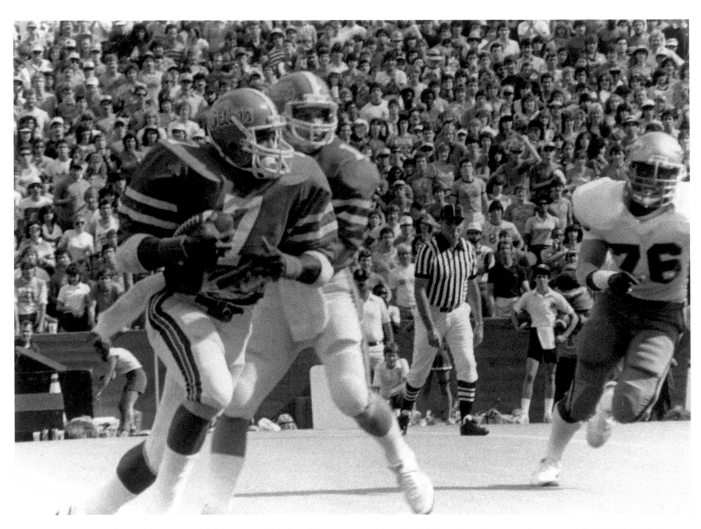

Lorenzo Hampton (no. 7) was one of the most effective Gator runners in the 1980s. As a four-year letterman (1981–1984), he rushed for nearly 2,000 yards. After UF, he was a first-round draft choice, playing for the Dolphins in the NFL (1985–1989).

UF president Marshall Criser and Head Coach Galen Hall, who replaced Charley Pell in 1984, hold the *New York Times* National Championship Trophy and the 1984 SEC Championship Trophy, both of which the team had won. The SEC took away the SEC Trophy in 1985 because of NCAA infractions. Galen Hall had a 40-18-1 record in his five and a half seasons (1984–1989).

In 1985, because the UF football program was on NCAA probation for violations during the Charley Pell era, the players and fans considered the annual game with rival FSU their "bowl" game. After the Gators had beaten the Seminoles, 38–14, for the fifth straight time, the players, including senior running back Neal Anderson, came out onto the field to thank the fans for their support.

As the team began to win consistently in the 1980s and 1990s, Florida Field sold out week after week. The newly built skyboxes brought in much revenue to the Athletic Association, as did the fees paid by major television studios wanting to broadcast the Gator games. The field was also used for the annual high school state championship game.

After a win, the Gators have celebrated before the media, in this case after a game in 1985 against FSU. More recently the athletes from both teams have gathered at midfield to say a prayer of thanks, especially if there were no serious injuries during the game. In the Urban Meyer era, the Gator players went to the student section to sing the alma mater with other students.

Emmitt Smith (no. 22) lettered at UF for three years (1987–1989). In 1988 he set school records for rushing yardage in one season (1,599), carries (284), rushing touchdowns (14), and rushing yards in one game (316 against New Mexico). After setting 58 school records, he left for the NFL after his junior year and starred for the Dallas Cowboys (1990–2002).

The coeds at UF who were part of the Twirlers or Dazzlers, as seen here in 1988, entertained the fans during halftime in the Swamp. They spent long hours practicing and traveling to away-games and were effective in rallying Gator fans in victories and in defeats.

Steve Spurrier, UF's first Heisman Trophy winner (1966), became the school's 19th head coach in 1990 and compiled an outstanding record of 102-21-1 in his time there (1990–2001). He had UF's second Heisman Trophy winner (Danny Wuerffel) and the school's first national championship team (1996). This photo shows him with the popular Florida governor Lawton Chiles. Spurrier has more recently coached in the NFL and at South Carolina.

Former Gator and Chicago Bears running back, Neal Anderson, returned to Florida Field in 1990 with his father, Tommy, to display a plaque commemorating their establishment of a women's tennis scholarship in honor of Neal's mother, Dorothy. Athletes like Neal Anderson have generously supported the university where they did so well.

Coach Spurrier brought many talents to the coaching ranks, including an enthusiasm that infected the players and crowd, innovations in a fun-'n'-gun offense, the determination to make Florida Field alien gridiron for opponents, and a desire instilled in many high school athletes to join him for exciting football. His insistence that workers replace the synthetic playing field with real grass probably helped mitigate many injuries to his players.

For more than 50 years George Edmondson, Jr., of Tampa, Florida, has been known as Mr. Two Bits for leading the fans in a "two bits" cheer from the middle of Florida Field. As shown here, he has also given scholarships to cheerleaders, some of the unsung heroes of Gator games.

An important academic issue for all college sports has been the graduation rate of athletes. Because the better athletes have sometimes left college for professional sports before they graduate, academic advisors do their best to encourage the athletes to earn degrees, even after leaving school. Here President John Lombardi congratulates football player Carlton Miles at the latter's graduation in 1992.

Coach Spurrier poses with his coaches and players from the 1993 SEC champion team during an outstanding 11-2 season. He is flanked by runner Errict Rhett (no. 33) and linebacker Ed Robinson (no. 41). The win over Alabama in December was UF's first win in the SEC championship game and a prelude to its win over West Virginia in the Sugar Bowl.

The national championship and other accomplishments would be repeated in 2006 and 2008 with the national championship win for Coach Urban Meyer's Gators. In both 1996 and 2006, the Gators won the championship despite having the toughest schedule, according to NCAA statistics. In 2007, quarterback Tim Tebow became the first sophomore to win the Heisman Trophy.

Notes on the Photographs

These notes, listed by page number, attempt to include all aspects known of the photographs. Each of the photographs is identified by the page number, a title or description, photographer and collection, archive, and call or box number when applicable. Although every attempt was made to collect all data, in some cases complete data may have been unavailable due to the age and condition of some of the photographs and records.

Printed in the USA
CPSIA information can be obtained
at www.ICGtesting.com
JSHW072026140824
68134JS00042B/3799